Worth Going Back

A Memoir of Alaska

John Williams

Copyright © 2018 John Williams
All rights reserved.
ISBN: 978-0-692-10561-0

Monday Creek Publishing LLC
mondaycreekpublishing.com

ACKNOWLEDGMENTS

Two people need to be thanked for this venture. First, to my wife Teddi for supporting me on this writing endeavor and having patience enough each evening to listen as I would read her my thoughts of the day. The thoughtful gesture of a blank journal from my son, Pete, was the motivation that got me started.

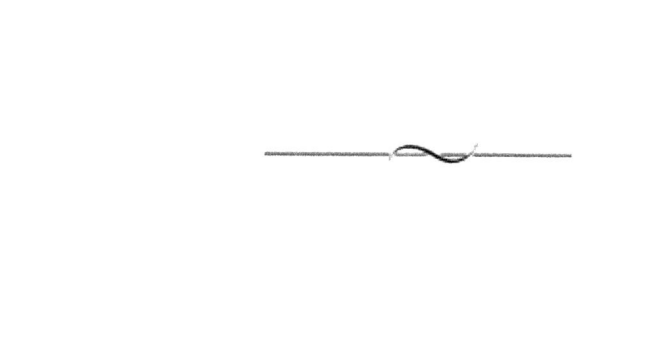

CAST OF CHARACTERS

	Relationship to...
Me, myself, I	John Williams
Teddi, Ma, Grandma	Wife
Mom	Mother
Dad	Father
Ticky	Uncle
George	Uncle
Naomi	Aunt
Heidi	Daughter
Kris	Son
Marcia	Daughter-in-law
Kristianna	Granddaughter
Wesley	Grandson
Isabel	Granddaughter
Josh	Son
Megan	Daughter-in-law
Katelyn	Granddaughter
Lindsay	Granddaughter
Pete	Son
Larry	Brother
Kathy	Larry's wife
Ronnie	Brother
Lea	Niece
Sharon	Sister
Beth	Sister
Jeff	Brother
Jo	Sister
Mark	Brother
Barb	Sister
Dean	Cousin
Virgialee	Dean's Wife
Mark	Virgialee's Brother

INTRODUCTION

Stories have to start somewhere, so this is my attempt at something I know nothing about. That would be putting on paper words that are readable yet have enough content to hold your interest. A year ago, Teddi thought about a vacation that would stretch beyond the usual family meetings yet give us time to connect with who we are and see things that might challenge us a little. When one goes into the unexpected, the heart rate goes up, but so does the anticipation of what lies ahead. We decided on driving to Alaska pulling our Trailmanor camper. We've pulled it across country on many occasions, but nothing like a trip to the northern reaches of our continent. Teddi researched all aspects of where we might travel to, also places to stop for food, supplies, gas stations, state or national parks, museums, monuments and the like. She spent a huge amount of time and effort to plan a route that would give us the best journey, yet not miss anything we would regret not seeing. Time was not going to be an issue. If we wanted to stop and see something, we would. If we had to turn around, we would. If we wanted to stay longer, we could. We both knew that not everyone has the opportunities to do such things and we are thankful for such a moment. Time, age, money, plus health are fleeting things and to get such to come together is a blessed thing.

Getting an automobile in good enough shape to travel many thousands of miles may not seem like a big thing, but to trust one with a quarter of a million miles on it already tests your faith. We carried the title with us for a worst-case scenario. Tires with enough tread to travel the distance were a concern, especially on the tire-eating camper. It was a civilized world we were heading into, not like a foreign land, so connecting with the locals didn't concern us. Parts could be an issue if the occasion arose, but that's an issue even in Southeast Ohio. Pete, our son, bought us a gas can for the journey and a can of bear spray. Where is his sense of adventure? Really, they were nice to have along.

The weather was a concern, especially leaving in the middle of July. I know you're thinking heat, but in my mind, snow would be the problem on mountain passes. After all, it's a land that stays frozen all of the time. It's where Santa lives. Glaciers grow in that part of the world. But adventure is what this family is all about, so we were expecting to be pushed a little. As the Colorado contingent would say, "we are a strong family."

As we begin this venture, some rules needed to be laid. It is not necessarily a journal of each day's activity or even where we travel, but something of the journey of that day may have reminded me of an experience from the past or maybe someone's other than mine. Thoughts came to mind that have nothing to do with much of anything other than maybe how I felt at a particular moment. Teddi inspires me to do more than I think I'm capable of, so sit back and see where the road leads. It may be a wild ride.

ALASKA BOUND

After years of travel we have seen a lot. Teddi and I have been on many adventures and most of them with our *kids*, but it would take another book to log all of their exploits. Many States have passed under our wheels, with only two remaining. Alaska is to be number 49 of the States to see. So, let's get started.

FRIDAY-SATURDAY, JULY 14-15

Our adventure starts from our beautiful home near Athens, Ohio. A short trip to Cedarville, Ohio, for a two-night stay with son Kris, Marcia, and family, kicked off this wandering. Kristianna showed and told of her classes and trip to Scotland. She was still excited. The next day we went to a farmer's market in Yellow Springs, Ohio. Marcia bought the best English muffins I've ever had. Kris seems to know all the good ice cream spots. This is corn and soybean country, not the heavily wooded area of home, but it has a beauty that farm areas display. We're excited to experience what the rest of our journey will show to us, so tomorrow it's off into the western sun we venture.

SUNDAY, JULY 16

This is still corn and soybean country and Indiana is similar to Ohio, but without the football prowess. Hoosier-land is a basketball world though and home of one of the great movies of all-time, *Hoosiers*. Farms seem to be a little larger.

MONDAY, JULY 17

We were awakened to the sound of nuts falling on our Trailmanor roof. Now I've heard many sounds of nature before while camping; like rain softly falling on our tin (actually aluminum) roof, or winds whistling through the cracks. Tornadoes have passed over us (really) at the Land Between the Lakes. Pine cones the size of small airplanes have come crashing through our fan vent. So anything bouncing off our roof gets our attention; today it was only small hickory nuts. Squirrels!

Today we visited Herbert Hoover's birth, burial, and museum site. All the years growing up listening to Dad rant on about the Hoover days are now questioned; not that it wasn't hard times, but that one man, even the President, was not at fault. Greed and poor judgement, plus a world stripped bare by war and a natural disaster thrown in were obstacles that took us to the starting point again. I also realized some of Roosevelt's achievements were actually started by Hoover. He enjoyed fly-fishing, so how bad could he be?

We're spending the night under an Iowa sky.

Tuesday, July 18

I think I have lived my life in a world that does not fit my nature. Southeast Ohio is a conglomeration of hills, valleys, twists and turns; add a little trash in each ravine and a few cars in the creek, and oh yeah, don't think of putting garbage in a container when you can throw it on the sidewalk or road, then you have where I live. But today in northwest Iowa I saw gently, ever so gently, rolling hills saturated with corn and soybeans with rows as straight as the previous inhabitant's arrows. We saw green fields and blue sky. Throw in a tall grass prairie with the flowers in bloom and one can get a feeling of reason and contentment. This country allows one to breathe with the feeling of a full breath, yes, I like open space, a horizon that takes time to see and a view that gives one time to think. Oh yeah, we saw bison today. We had ice cream at the self-proclaimed ice cream capital of the world. It's been a good day.

Wednesday, July 19

Today I had a chance to go back in time; a time when life was much simpler. I could have been a kid playing in a small stream or running in the fields with my brothers and sisters, or maybe even throwing rocks at trees. At night I could have stretched out on my back and looked for shooting stars. My Dad could be picking at stone in a mine; my Mother cooking supper. It may sound like my childhood, but in reality, it was an Indian's life in Blue Stone of South Dakota. Simplicity is good.

Thursday, July 20

Have you ever went anywhere and asked yourself, why does this place exist? Sturgis, South Dakota is that kind of place. There are bars the size of ballrooms and ten times more than a town should have, and all for a week or two out of the year. Their client's come hundreds to thousands of miles to join in on the party. To think, we annihilated a culture of merit to do such things. That sounds too negative, so I'll add the good I had today. I love open space; today's landscape took away all trees and showed me grass and wheat as far as my eyes let me see. Yes, the air traveled with a good pace, but not like yesterday, when it flattened cornstalks and moved rain horizontally. After hours of no civilization and no coffee, we finally came to a small town. Surprisingly, it had a really upscale coffee shop. Not just any run of the mill shop, but one that sold Wrangler jeans, plus about anything one needed. A young lady waited on me. As I have noticed in my travels, young people in farm areas are above the average scale in social skills. We spoke of travel and other things, but we discussed the difference between ranchers and farmers. If you're west of the Mississippi River and have cattle, you're a rancher, but east of the same river, you'll probably be growing something in the ground, even if you have cattle, then you're a farmer. Ranchers are above farmers in this western world. The girl's family was the first to settle the land, and she grew up playing in streams and wondered if other little girls from other cultures did the same.

We camped on the Spearfish Canyon Highway in South Dakota after a day of wheat fields and grassland.

Friday, July 21

Have you ever had a day when your expectations didn't quite jive with what you planned? We were entering Montana today and I know how beautiful the country is from previous trips, but fires in the surrounding area left a lingering smoke screen. We planned on camping on the Bear Tooth Highway, but not actually take it to Yellowstone. This drive rivals any I've seen for scenic beauty. All designated sites were full, so we turned around and headed back toward Red Lodge. As we came around a bend, I spotted an RV top across a river in an open field. We crossed a bridge and found many RV's in the same spot. While setting up camp I noticed we were surrounded by sharp peaks, and a roaring stream nearby. As we were eating our evening meal, I could hear the sound of music. My first thought was someone was playing a radio, but it seemed better. I stepped out the door to see where it was coming from when an older fellow walked by with a chair and asked me to go sit and listen to some music with him. So I did. A band of seven; six guys and one girl were playing old time country music. Brother Ronnie would have loved it. The girl on an upright bass, two mandolin pickers, two guitars, one banjo, and one fiddle. The fiddle player was good as one could get. The others were really good also. Some knew each other, some did not, but they played and sang as good as any group that tours together. The day was not as I expected, but finished better than planned.

SATURDAY, JULY 22

Today's drive is to take us up the Missouri River following the Lewis and Clark route. That to me was the adventure of adventures; just a small group seeing things new every day, and in the most natural way that was possible. Have you ever been to a car show? Red Lodge, Montana, lines the streets with old restored cars for blocks. What a contrast from the time of Corp of Discovery. One never knows what one may see on a trip of adventure.

Sunday, July 23

Around fifty years ago I was in Glacier National Park with Larry and Kathy. I hiked to a ridgeline that overlooked Iceberg Lake. Today it looked a long way off, but then just a morning stroll. Fear is learned as years go by. Fear of trying keeps people from some great adventures. Fear makes the heart pump. As I was gazing at the trail I took years ago, I saw two grizzly bears moving along the mountainside. To see grizzly on a trail is a story I hope I could write about after the fact, if I was on that trail; I've learned fear.

Monday-Friday, July 24-28

Most people succeed in business by taking

chances. You plan for the best but, sometimes it just doesn't pan out. Today we got up early so maybe we could get a campsite in Glacier National Park. People are seeking to escape the clutter, comfort and technology for a more natural way; if only for a few days. National Parks are filled to the brim with those people. As a result, the Parks are extremely crowded. Our quest for a campsite could have turned out like so many; *campground full,* but it did not. While waiting our turn for a site, a fellow stopped and said he was leaving and had a spot on the water. We checked it out. Now, I don't play the lottery, but this site was like hitting the jackpot. A lake emptying into a mountain stream, which was surrounded by peaks, that was supplying the very water going by. Josh, Megan, Katelyn and Lindsay met us there. We hiked to Hidden Lake on Logan Pass. Montana flowers were out everywhere. We walked through snow and saw mountain goats. It was a good day. The next was to be a relaxing day. The Core Board paddle board came out along with some smaller ones for the kids, and I rented a kayak and we were welcomed by Two Medicine Lake. If there is a more beautiful lake to paddle on, I haven't found it yet. Oh yeah, last evening's Ranger talk on *birdies* was hilarious and educational - *Wiggle Verm*! Bighorn sheep were on a trail to Appistoki Waterfall. A momma black bear with two cubs traversed the hillside across from camp. An extremely large trout swam by just at dark.

The next day found us on the north fork of the Flathead River rafting. What a great family river. We talked, laughed, and just plain had a good time. At other places we saw many beautiful settings. Five days later we reluctantly moved on. Yes, we moved on; north toward Alaska.

SATURDAY, JULY 29

We're crossing the line today. I've done that a few times in my life and wished I hadn't. Like backtalking to my Dad. When he picked up a nearby ball bat and stepped toward me, I realized

I had crossed that line. My next thought was feet don't fail me now. Adventures! Aren't they great? Canada should be a good line to cross.

SUNDAY, JULY 30

Today I realized how small I am in relation to the earth I live in. Passing the Waldron Ranch, which happens to be the largest in Alberta, I got a feel for what the Great Plains was once like. Grassland stretching far into the hills; belly deep to a cow. Scattered clouds as far as the eye can see. Then we started heading up the Kananaskis Highway going north. Now, my smallness was not horizontal, but vertical. We saw rocky mountainsides reaching for the clouds; formations of rocks that make no sense. A little like the lives of most people. Yet our lives are intermingled with nature more than we like to think. The trees are beginning to have a more northerly appearance, now.

MONDAY, JULY 31

I have a question! Why, when things aren't

done the way we like, we act in a negative way and sometimes we're not very nice about it? Camping seems to bring out a lot of negative vibes in some people. Someone's driving too fast or playing music too loud, etc. A little education goes a long way. Respect is a lost trait that needs to return. Know the rules before you get into the game or it's like Saturday morning at Ohio University's Grover Center on the ball court. A few standoffs and everyone gets educated. I miss those days. I'm guessing my kids do, too.

Mountains saturated with smoke today. Fires in British Columbia are affecting the landscape for hundreds, if not thousands of miles. It's a different look, but still spectacular. If you have ever been to a zoo, you could relate to today's activity. Forty some years ago we visited Banff and Lake Louise; both were beautiful and even tranquil. Today is where the zoo comes in. Traffic was at a standstill. Kind of like watching a monkey perform in its cage and everyone stops to see what is going on. A lake filled with rented boats, and masses at lake's edge. The mountains are still there with the glaciers, but the tranquil feeling not.

We're camping along a flowing river among the spruce with mountain peaks around us. It's a nice campsite.

TUESDAY, AUGUST 1

It's been reported or claimed that the Ice Fields Highway is the most beautiful drive in the world. Now; I've seen the Tetons, Yellowstone, Bear Tooth Highway, the Olympics of Washington, Mt. Rainier, Oregon Coast, Big Sur, Blue Ridge, and other stunning places, but the Ice Fields claim is dead on. I'm not saying that the claim is completely true; so I'll be looking for other places that may beat what I've seen. It may be a challenge, but challenges are what Williams' are all about. Running marathons, Spartan Races, skiing the outer limits, swimming in Lake Michigan, floating the Gauley River, living in New York, living in Florida, and doing triathlons, just to name a few. The skiing movie maker, Warren Miller, always says that "if you don't do it today, you will be another day older when you do." It was a spectacular day. I can't wait for tomorrow.

WEDNESDAY, AUGUST 2

Today's journey has taken us from the mountains to the prairie. Along the way I've seen the reason southeast Ohio people are fighting the oil and gas boom so. The city and surrounding areas of Grande Prairie is a mecca of gas and oil activity. It's an industrial sprawl that seems to have no plans of sustaining life after the wells go dry. But on a lighter side, we visited the site of a town that Teddi's ancestral cousin started. He was banking on a railroad to pass through his settlement, but it went south instead, so it never happened. But, to his credit, he started the idea of raising grain in such a northern location. Sometimes one has to see the past to understand the person.

I remember going up the back forty chasing cows to bring back to milk, and sitting on a high point looking as far as I could see and imagine what could possibly be beyond. So my past fascination with the beyond has brought me to the upper reaches of Canada. I'm still imagining what's beyond.

THURSDAY, AUGUST 3

Not everyone gets the opportunity to go to zero and start over again. Choosing Christ can do that when we have messed up the first go round, but this is not a religious message. Yet, that can be a life-changing adventure. Have I said adventures are good? Today in Dawson Creek British Columbia we started out at zero on the Alaskan Highway. Before the adventure started we each posed for photos at the milepost sign like the rest of the highway travelers. We checked out a museum at the welcome center. Looking at all the artifacts made me realize I'm awful old or I grew up with some awful old stuff. I had seen or used about all the antiques around the house or someplace. A homemade snowmobile caught my eye. It took me back to when Larry had built a motorbike from an old bicycle. He also made some sort of soapbox from boards and wheels. Put those two together and it would resemble the snowmobile. Teddi tried to pick up a Mammoth bone but couldn't budge it. An article was on display about her cousin Ancel Maynard Bezanson starting a grain farming industry in this northern country; that was kind of cool.

Friday, August 4

Tomorrow we'll be crossing the line into Yukon Territory. Years ago many came seeking to get rich by panning for gold. It's an unbelievably long trek. So long, I'm not sure how they could do it. I'm not really strapped for time, but those people didn't have automobiles like I do. I guess the saying *where there is a will there is a way* fits those that came.

We saw stone sheep today; that was new to

me. We've been looking for caribou, but none have been spotted yet. A young black bear caught our eye this morning as it was running next to the road. We're camped on the Trout River tonight with the sound of glacier water soothing our ears.

SATURDAY, AUGUST 5

Marketing something tells of all the good points. It may be by words or pictures. I've seen many a brochure of the Yukon before I ever left home, so I had in my mind what it might be like. If you relish the urban world, this place will not impress you. If many miles bore you, it's not your territory. With all that said, I find it one of the prettiest places I've been. The air is pure and the sky scattered with the whitest of clouds. I took a few deep breaths to clear any toxins in my lungs; then I felt guilty for polluting the air around me. It's natural; it's just as it's always been. There are valleys, and hills, with the rivers softly twisting their way towards the different oceans. The animals move slowly; maybe they are telling us something we don't know. I actually looked forward to seeing the Yukon more than Alaska. It has not disappointed. Today we saw wood bison and another beautiful black bear. It's been another good day.

S‌unday, A‌ugust 6

This is to be a rest day on this adventure. We traveled a few miles with an early camp planned. We watched salmon making their last voyage at a fish ladder. Also splurged at an outdoor dining house and toured the S.S. Klondike. Then spent the afternoon in my hammock, under the Sitka spruce; tall slender trees with branches that protrude only short distances from their trunk. It's a species known for making great acoustical instruments. I ask myself why; why this type of wood for a fine sounding guitar? It's straight grained for sure, and light as a feather. As I understand, the cellular make-up is what generates the great sound, but watching it sway back and forth in the gentle breeze, I'm thinking it's tuned by nature. The sound of thunder on the mountain peaks in the distance gives it that robust tone. But what do I know. I live where wood is hard and heavy.

MONDAY, AUGUST 7

I remember as a kid going to either Lake Hope or Old Man's Cave. Mom and Dad put us in the back of Uncle Tick's flatbed truck. We pretty well filled it up because there were so many of us. Going anywhere was always exciting for me. Ticky and George always had the greatest vehicles. I remember Tick's red '57 Chevy convertible with black interior and a white top. He also had a twelve-cylinder Hudson, or it may have been a Packard, I'm not sure. Larry seems to think it was a Zephyr. He also had a car that you had to start off with a clutch, but after that it was automatic. George had a '54 Lincoln Capri coupe that was out of this world. Those were exciting times.

Today was exciting also. Ma and myself took the White Pass-Yukon train over the White Pass which is famous for the Chilkoot Trail that took gold seekers north to Dawson Creek, a five-hundred-mile journey. It's a narrow gage rail that traverses some really difficult terrain, but some of the most beautiful. Today's route connects Skagway, Alaska, with Frazer, British Columbia. It's ranked in the top ten train rides in the world. I think Ma and myself felt like kids again. This was a really good day.

Tuesday, August 8

Sun continues to shine in the Yukon. We've been spoiled by endless clear sunny days and cool nights for great sleeping. I'll tap on my woody head so not to change our good fortune. It's a land that has drawn young people from faraway places to live. Not many in numbers, but many with the heart to just live life at the fullest. I really like what I've seen as we've traveled through the Yukon. It's the gold I was looking for.

Wednesday, August 9

One more hour of daylight; that means we

have driven across the boundary into Alaska. If your life is so busy and you think you need more time, this is the place for you. It never gets dark, or that's as it seems. I force myself to bed, even though it appears there are a few more hours of daylight, thinking I could get a few more things done. But this is a land that getting one more thing done doesn't seem that important. Kind of like childhood days when you were outside playing and Mom would tell you to come in because it was getting dark, and you did, because tomorrow you could do it all over again.

The vastness of this world never ceases to amaze me. We saw snow white peaks that had to be one hundred miles away. White Trumpeter swans feeding in a lake, pumice saturated rivers a mile wide, flowing toward the Yukon. Just for Megan, both Ma and I went swimming in an Alaskan lake to prove that we've got a little adventuring left in us. I try to always have fun and enjoy what life gives me; I'm thankful I've been given a lot, may your lot be full also.

Thursday, August 10

Have you ever run out of gas? Not the physical kind, or the mental kind, because we have all done that, but the kind you put in your auto or truck. If not, you're missing out on some great adventures. I've run out a few times, but they have led to some great stories. One of my first times was when pulling two weeks of military summer camp in Yakima, Washington. I had finished my two weeks and was heading back to Seattle. I was traveling over White Pass, then Cyuse Pass on my way back. If you have ever been in the Cascade Mountains you know how beautiful they are. Less than one hundred yards from the top of Cyuse Pass the engine quit, the gas gauge needle below empty. I had a pretty efficient car but forgot to check the gauge. That was the car that turned Teddi's head, so I could reel her in. It was a 1967 Triumph Spitfire, bright red, had knock off wire wheels, and three different tops. One was a removable hard top, one a fold back soft top, and one that just exposed the driver. I loved that car! It was also very light. I thought I could push it over the pass. I couldn't. It was one of those spectacular days. The sun was out, the sky blue, snow-capped peaks in all directions, Mount Rainier right beside me. I sat down near the car and was taking in the sights, sounds, and smells of such a perfect setting. An hour later the first vehicle came by. To my surprise, he had a can of gas. I paid and thanked him for the fuel. I actually hated to leave, but being AWOL wasn't a good idea.

I've been out of gas twice in Wyoming and both with my daughter Heidi along. She was just a baby the first time; same car. I could see the station, although it was miles away. A fellow stopped and gave me a ride and also after hearing my story of a wife and baby left behind, gave me a ride back. Many years later the same three were going over the Continental Divide. We were out of gas again. Heidi wasn't happy; adulthood does that to you. But I rode my bicycle over the divide in both directions. That was fun.

Today in Alaska I didn't run out of gas, but came closer than I should have. More beautiful scenes today, dust devils on a dry lake and saw the Alaskan Pipeline. It's a great adventure.

Friday, August 11

Today we went to the North Pole. The farthest point north on our journey, and yes, there is a Santa Claus. It's the first cloudy day we've had in four weeks, but still pretty nice. We looked around Fairbanks to get a feel for this city's lifestyle. It's a little haphazard but not much different than any small American city. If you like old cars, really nice old cars, the Fountainhead Antique Auto Museum is the place to see. American-made automobiles from 1898 to the 1930's are on display, around 78 of them. Most still run and some are the only ones in existence. Along with the autos, there is clothing, men's and women's, from each era next to the car on display. Auto styles have receded a long way from these beauties of the past. Frankly, so have dress styles of both male and female. We had a feast at the Alaskan Salmon Bake Restaurant. You walk through a replica of a mine tunnel to get to an outside all-you-can-eat site of salmon, cod, prime rib, and all the stuff on any food bar. Ma and myself went away as full as ticks. It's after 10:00 PM and the sun still hasn't set yet, but I'm ready to set myself in bed. It's been a fine day.

SATURDAY, AUGUST 12

Today's venture has brought us to Denali National Park and Preserve. If you have never been here, you have no idea how large it is. Tomorrow we're taking a shuttle towards the inside of the park. Ours is going to stop at mile post 66. We could go two stops farther, with the last at 92 miles. This is one-way folks, and it's not halfway through the park. There is a reason it's called a Preserve. We drove a few miles into the park today and saw willow ptarmigan, and caribou. A system has moved in and it's raining, so a view of Denali may not happen. Only 25 to 35% of people who visit get to see it anyway. We're planning on being around a few days, so maybe it will pop out. To put in perspective, it's like going to a major pro-athletic event and getting tickets in the top tier, your chances of seeing any number on a uniform are somewhere between slim and none, if you can even see the players, and chances are you're a few hundred bucks lighter in the process.

SUNDAY, AUGUST 13

A friendly female Ranger asked us today to think of what the wilderness means to me as a person. As she was talking to us and challenging our thoughts of the wilderness, I felt the passion of a person who has dedicated her life to save and pass on the natural world to us, our children, grandchildren, and their grandchildren. Maybe to deaf ears for some, but her heart and mine were united.

I remember taking a picture, at a pullout in the Grand Tetons on one of my first trips through that park. Years later Pete showed me a picture he had taken as he remembered from seeing my photo at the exact same view. Only in National Parks is that going to happen. It's why the world comes to the United States to visit our parks.

Today we saw the mountains, the valleys, glacial remains, trees, tundra, and mist over the peaks; bear, Dall sheep, caribou, wolverine, snowshoe rabbits, ptarmigan, and many smaller birds and animals, plus snow at higher elevations with crevices. As the Ranger challenged me about passing this amazing creation on, I am as humbled as she was that we can see, feel, smell, and hear the heartbeat of nature that has been passed down to us. Yes, it's been a good day.

Monday, August 14

Permafrost is a roadbuilders nightmare. In this northern country they actually try to keep it frozen so it won't move so much. The best way I can describe their roads is for you to drive any road in Athens County. It's not bad, but it's not good either. A lady shuttle driver, commented on one of our trips, that it took just a little over eight months in 1942 to build 1,400 miles of the Alaskan Highway, but it takes a year now to fill a pothole.

Things in your path kind of get you by surprise. A little like tiger pits. Katelyn, Lindsay, and Isabel are master tiger pit builders. On a Michigan camping trip they dug a hole and covered it with sticks, grass, and moss. But since there are no tigers in Michigan, their chances of a big catch seemed small. But low and behold the trap was sprung. The noise and thrashing sent the signal they had a good catch. Everyone ran to see. Sadly, it was not a tiger but only Grandma. What a great camping trip.

A mist today as we head south. It's mostly uninhabited, but a village every now and then. Vegetation is getting thicker and trees have moss hanging from the limbs; a sign of moisture in the air. We've got a nice hiking trail beside Byers Lake, near our camping spot for the night. A couple had built a cabin overlooking the lake in 1959. The land has almost reclaimed it, but the setting has not changed; it's beautiful.

A little rain tonight; it'll be good for sleeping. We're taking our time while the weather stays cloudy, as not to miss any of the great views that are all around us. Ma ate an Alaskan blueberry; she said it was bitter. She's spoiled by the Maine blueberry, I think. It's been a pleasant day and camp.

TUESDAY, AUGUST 15

How far would you ride a bicycle? A couple of blocks, or maybe a few miles and probably on a paved bike path. On a really good day, you might ride to the closest town from your home. This venture has opened my eyes to what endurance means. We could be in the middle of a 150 mile stretch of nothing but wilderness, away from towns with populations of 10 to 20, when we'll pass a lone person on a bicycle. The surprising thing is that it may be a female. Our world is so regulated by what should be or shouldn't be done; that when I see something contrary to the norm, I'm a little surprised. I'm beginning to believe more and more, it was the female that was the driving force when pursuing adventure. Alaska is large enough for everyone, both male and female, I'm glad I'm here.

Today we set our wheels on the Kenai Peninsula. The mountains with the valleys of ice spread out in front of us bathed in sunlight. We made camp as two girls were heading to a nearby stream with their kayaks for a paddle. Somewhere in the conversation, they told me it wasn't a stream but a creek. I suppose if I was in the Adirondacks, they would tell me it was a brook. Men are lined up shoulder to shoulder, where the salt water and fresh water collide, trying to snag a salmon. It's a wonder any make it to the spawning grounds at all. Today's sights were not of animals but of lakes, bays, flowers, mountains, glaciers, and a much denser forest. We passed through Anchorage today. It may be hard to believe but it's the first so called city since Indianapolis we've encountered in a month of travel. If you've been to one city, you have been to them all. US cities have no character. I'm eager for what tomorrow will bring us.

WEDNESDAY, AUGUST 16

Yesterday's site of fishermen on the riverbank brought back memories of fishing on the banks of the Hocking River. Dad would take us to some choice spots where the carp would hang out. I never remember Dad catching a fish, but it was fun just to go. On one particular trip, Dad had prepared some doughballs for the occasion. No fish in its right mind would pass up such a tasty morsel so finely prepared; and they probably didn't. The problem was that they wouldn't stay on the hook. You cast your line out and the doughball went flying. On another trip with Dad, Larry, Sharon, and myself, I'm not sure if Beth or Ronnie was along, but we went to a really good hot spot where the city's sewers emptied into the river. Big carp were always around those spots. Larry wasn't getting any hits where he was, so he was moving to a better place. He stepped in a muddy spot and into the river he went. You guessed it, right where the sewer emptied into the river. He was a little embarrassed, but we were the ones that paid the price of smelling him all the way home. He got hosed off before Mom would let him in the house. What a great fishing trip.

Today's trips to Kenai, on the shores of Cook Inlet, were quite rewarding. More fishermen on the banks and in boats occupied several rivers on the way. Kenai is a fishing town plus an oil town. We saw several platforms in the bay; one real close to the shore. They're really large. We stopped at the visitor's center and saw a display of turned woodwork. I see what they do in the winter here. We got a tip on a seafood restaurant and it turned out far above the average. Actually, the best Halibut I've eaten, so that was good. We went down a pothole road in a quest to find

Moose but only found some blue bonnet flowers. Tonight, the heater's on and rain gently falling on the roof; the world has gotten a lot simpler, and that's good, too.

Thursday, August 17

Forty-nine years ago I united with the greatest person on earth. On that day the true adventure began. We have raised four to adulthood and couldn't be prouder of who they have become. They are great people with great character. Along the way they have added six of their own with another on the way; I also see quality in each of them. Teddi gets all the credit, because she had to raise me also. I'm sure I was in the way a lot. We've lived our life with as much adventure as time and money allowed. It has allowed a lot. We have been blessed beyond measure. As of today we have seen every state except Hawaii and every Canadian Province but the Northwest Territories, and it's all been fun, but the true adventure is growing with your children. As they grow, you grow also. Sure, somedays were challenging, but each day worth the ride. Ma is the best person I have ever known. I think Angels take lessons from her. I could go on and on but more stories are waiting to be told, like what we experienced today.

That would be Exit Glacier and Alaska Sea Life Center. The Center gave us a great look of the marine life that inhabits this part of the world; from the seals and Steller sea lions, a baby Walrus, all the fish species, to the puffins and things that resemble plants but are not. It was a great display. That afternoon we made the two and half mile trek to Exit Glacier and back. It's the only one you can drive close too. Once up close you can see how large they really are; we're just specs among towering ice. Ma did great; I think she is training for a marathon in a couple of decades. It's late and my down sleeping bag is calling.

FRIDAY, AUGUST 18

Westward ho! Today our journey took us to

the western most point one can drive in North America. That spot is Anchor Point. It was on our way to Homer, which was our destination. I believe we have driven to the most easterly and westerly points of this Northern American Continent. Now we'll have to set our goals that stretch beyond our boundaries. At the price of food and gas here we are stretching George a long way; oh yeah, and don't forget about the Queen. It's a small price for such an adventure. We saw some massive glaciers today across the Kachemak Bay. We drove out to Homer Spit and took in some shops and had lunch. The salmon and clams were good and the scenery was even better. We looked out across the Bay with fishermen and probably fisherwomen in their boats going after the big ones. Beyond that, mountains with their valleys filled with ice. Yes, it's cool here; probably in the low 50's to high 40's. Yesterday we could see fresh snow on the higher peaks. It has an autumn, maybe early winter feel if compared to southeast Ohio. Style is not an issue here;

whatever keeps you warm is vogue. If you are a fisherman, this is fish heaven, it has so many places to throw a line in and truly expect to get something in return. It was a long drive today, but interesting. We're moving camp tomorrow as to be closer to Anchorage. We'll try to make contact with cousin Dean before starting our venture back south.

SATURDAY, AUGUST 19

Have you ever been disappointed in something - I mean expecting this great moment, or event, or sight that would send you into ecstasy? Ma was talking about the Blueberry Festival at Alyeska Ski Area, pretty much all day. You have to know how much this lady likes blueberries to understand the anticipation of such an event. She not only likes them, but I think she is the world's foremost expert in how a blueberry should taste. Coming from Maine, her palate is tuned to that sweet savory taste, and that thought gets her excited. I did say she likes blueberries.

Well, we arrive and intermingle with the crowds to take it all in. We stroll through the booths of displays, the artist sections, the food vendors, and hear the sound of music from the stage area. I'm now seeing a lot of concern on her face; she turns and says, "There is nothing hear with blueberries, nothing." There was just one table which had blueberry pie that had long since been sold out. Sadness comes when you least expect it. We left. But all was not lost, as we found an ice cream shop along the road on the way back to camp that had real Alaskan blueberries. I wiped a tear from her eye and a smile came to her face.

We went through a long railroad tunnel today with our car. It's the only tunnel in North America that shares its space. No cosmetics here; just bare walls with boards on each side of the tracks to run on. It's a one-lane affair, so you have to wait your turn. It comes out at Whittier on Prince William Sound. It's not the most scenic port, but on the inland side of the tunnel is Portage Bay, which is about as scenic as it gets. It's a glacial lake surrounded by mountains with valleys filled with glaciers. It even has icebergs floating in the water. Yes, another good day.

Sunday, August 20

Our camp today is in Williwaw National Forest. A high mountain valley beside us with waterfalls tumbling down all over, the near vertical walls tower above us with snow fields clinging near its top, with glaciers here and there. It's been raining and the sound of rain on our roof is quite soothing. Not traveling today which was preplanned, so the rain is nice. It's a day to catch up on the little things and organize a little also.

Have you ever been on a rafting trip? They do a lot of rafting here in Alaska. They transport people, they have scenic float trips, and they fish out of them; they do whitewater rafting. I was standing on a riverbank near Denali a while back watching a family prepare for a trip. I was talking to their guide about the trip which was a class 2 float of around 10 miles. In our conversation he mentioned about half their guides were from West Virginia. It brought memories back of a few trips of my own; like one on the Gauley River with Josh, Pete, Eddie or Jim or whatever his name was, and I. They come from all over the world to Denali, but they also come from all over the world to run the Gauley River in the fall season. It's not any class-two float but a river with five-plus falls; like Sweet Falls, that's the name of the rapid. It's where the outfitters sit on rocks, eating their lunch, while others try to navigate the stream, for the show. We gave them one with a standing ovation, or I should say Josh and Pete did. Eddie, Jim, or whatever his name is, and I ran it perfect. Josh and Pete misjudged their route and flipped coming over the falls. Our rafts were not self-bailing, so they filled with water. After flipping, raft, bodies and all went into a box canyon where their raft became pinned against a rock wall while completely submerged. We're talking 13-foot rafts here. Josh and Pete climbed on the rock the raft was pinned against; as a parent, it's a big relief knowing your children are safe. That's when our raft floated around the corner and out of sight. We paddled to shore as to go up the bank to help them out. The sound I heard then caught me by surprise and a little dumbfounded; a cheer by throngs of people which echoed off the canyon walls. As the story goes, Josh was tugging at the raft when it finally popped up, right side up filled with water. Josh stepped in as it was floating away. Pete was farther up the rock watching when a guide sitting on the bank mentioned, "Aren't you going with your raft?" Pete took a run and jumped. He landed with a cannonball in the middle as it floated by. The crowd loved it, and that's why the ovation. Memories are not just ours, but for many others.

Many salmon that filled a nearby stream was our only outside sights today, except torrents of raindrops falling from heaven. Salmon, migrating, is an amazing site, only equaled by a paddle trip in Michigan. That's a story for tomorrow.

Monday, August 21

This is granddaughter Isabel's great adventure. Camping leaves us with a lot of stories, like meeting Josh, Megan, Katelyn, and Lindsay in western Michigan, and paddling a small stream in our kayaks. Isabel and Heidi were along with us. The stream moved fairly fast so we thought this would be a quick trip. Isabel with me, and others paired young with an adult. Heidi was paddling solo. The current would push my boat with Isabel into the brush along the edge of the stream on about all curves, not because I'm a poor seaman (maybe), but because of boat design. She got tired of me hitting her in the head with my paddle, so switched boats with Katelyn. The lighter cargo helped a little. This short float started to become not so short. Nightfall was looming on the horizon; salmon were appearing under our boats, and then dead ones on banks and at shallow spots. Their life cycle had come to an end. At one particular rapid Heidi and I overturned; we pulled our boats to shore and the others stopped also. Fatigue had set in and nerves a little on edge. We were all standing around on the bank with decaying fish everywhere. All was pretty quiet when Heidi let's out with a burst, "*I hate the smell of death.*" Silence again, then interrupted by Megan's laughter, followed by the rest of us. Heidi then says "*what...*". The situation was then back under control and the take out came soon after. It was a trip to remember.

We had a short drive today to Anchorage. It cleared enough that we could see snow covered mountains toward the north; possibly Denali, but I'll have to check my coordinates, if so a rare sighting. Dean is flying in tomorrow from a trip to the lower 48. We'll get together in a day or two, I'm sure.

Tuesday, August 22

I expected homes in Alaska to be more picturesque than most are; a southeast Ohio home in general would be really nice here. Yet, some log ones are really quaint; even some with plants on their roof growing out of the dirt. Also some have a small log structure on stilts close to the house for food storage to keep bears from taking their supply. But rarely a home as nice as Kris and Marcia has in Yellow Springs. Log homes are rustic; especially the outside appearance, but they have a warm, homey feel on the inside. Shops and restaurants utilize that feel with a wood burning stove in the middle of the room; not for show but for real warmth. I'm sure the homes are no exception because of the huge piles of wood stacked outside the back door.

If you have never built a house, you should. It'll test about any skill you think you have, if you love playing in the dirt that's a good place to start. If you like swinging in midair, you'll love hanging from rafters. If pain excites you, a couple of blows with a hammer will cure you of that. If those don't charge you up, a hot electrical wire might, or how about a summersault off the roof to an unfinished porch below; ask Kris about that one. If you have a nurse for a wife, I guess it's worth a try. When the piece's start to come together, and the finishing trim goes up, it's a pretty good moment. All my clan has built, rebuilt or remodeled their homes. Skills that are not common to most people. Love is the ingredient that really makes a home, not the parts. Yesterday, I mentioned the pouring rain and the salmon; today I stopped again to take pictures of such an awesome sight. They were still there by the droves, but kind of sad watching the final stage of their lives. Once they spawn, which shows more caring than I expected, they quit eating and die. Only after beating the odds to get to that point does life begin anew.

Dreams do come true. Today the skies cleared and Denali could be seen from Anchorage; not just through clouds, but in its entirety. There was some haze in the air from all the rain we've had, but still clear; if looking at something from 130 miles away could be clear. That moves us over the zero to 25% that gets to see this amazing mountain; from base to top it's the tallest mountain in the world, surpassing Everest. We checked out a lot of the sites throughout the city of Anchorage today. We visited a site from the 1964 earthquake that slid into Cook Inlet, and saw a monument of Captain James Cook, the greatest explorer-navigator the world has known. He was a farmhand's son from Yorkshire, England. We went to an Ulu knife factory; a tool the native Alaskans used. We made contact with Dean and going to his place tomorrow evening. For being in a city, I would still call this a pretty good day.

WEDNESDAY, AUGUST 23

Have you ever stood at the end of an airport runway and watched airplanes take off or land? Yesterday, in Anchorage, we were at a spot near where planes take off and land. Cars were parked near the fence of what they call the blast zone. It's exciting for those that are there. I remember Larry taking me to a fence where the planes came in at Sea-TAC Airport. As the planes approached the runway on arriving you could see the eyes of the pilots; the planes were not many feet above your head, as the flaps were down, and the wheels locked in place with the engines roaring. What a rush! Larry loved it; he would get really hyper when they passed overhead. I'd get a little excited myself.

We are camping tonight on the Eagle River. We went to Dean and Virgialee's for dinner. Salmon was the course with new potatoes, Alaskan broccoli, cabbage, with ice cream and cookies out of the oven for dessert. They have a beautiful log home at timberline with a view out of this world. We had a good visit and met Virgialee's brother, Mark. He's a really nice fellow who's into genealogy big time. He showed us a picture of Larry in his Ohio University basketball uniform that I've never seen, and to top this day off we saw two Moose; one a nice bull.

Thursday, August 24

Our visit with Dean and Virgialee, plus her brother Mark yesterday was a real joy. Hearing his stories of past remembrances and where he is today was heartwarming; from his talking of his parents to ours. He mentioned of coming to my Mom and Dad's house while in college: Mom would say "come on in, take your coat off, your shirt if you like." He remembered how hot Dad kept it in the house. Then Mom would say, "Sit down and I'll get you something to eat." Dean called her the salt of the earth. He remembered the closeness my parents shared. Virgialee, after hearing our stories, can't wait to meet the rest of the family. I asked Dean how he came to settle in Alaska. He said after college he came for the summer. Like so many that came here he got the bug and never wanted to leave. He spoke of his job and how blessed and humbled he is to have the chance to make a difference in people's lives. He spoke of Virgialee as a God send. He's just a man content to be where he is; but life moves on and today, so did Teddi and myself. This is the turning point in our trip; the point from leaving home to the point of coming back. It's been six weeks since we left, it may take even longer to get back. No, we are not homesick, but a little warmth would feel pretty good about now. We are camped at the base of the Matanuska Glacier; literally; that's why heat would feel good. The awesome scenery never ends. Today we visited the only Musk Ox farm in the world and learned all about their history. These can never roam wild, but there are some in northern Alaska that do. Farther up the road more Moose; after a long dry spell they are cropping up everywhere. It's been a good day; actually a good six weeks.

Friday, August 25

Have you ever built a dam? Any kid that's ever been by a stream probably has. We've seen a lot of water after arriving in Alaska, but most are natural lakes or bays; sometimes a manmade dam but not many. Katelyn and Lindsay never miss a chance to stop flowing water; there Dad, Josh, was one of the great dam builders. I remember all of us kids on Long Run at one time or another tried to halt our water from going anywhere else. Larry was an engineer, but he was a dam builder first. The first branch off Long Run upstream from the old home place was forced to stop flowing by one of his projects. He cut trees down, then stood the post on end and wired them together with a little clay mud to fill the gaps. It worked great until the first gully washer, and like so many government projects, failed the test. I was lucky; when I was in my water stopping prime, the spoil bank from the strip mine slid into the creek and made a great lake on Coal Branch in back of our house. I built a raft and thought I was Tom Sawyer. The problem was is that it was all in the shade and the water never warmed much; still it was a great summer until it eventually washed out. As a kid, life is fun, I can't wait to grow up and see what else life unfolds. Autumn has arrived in central Alaska. Nights are nippy and foliage is starting to take on the fall colors. An 84-mile round trip in the Wrangell-St. Elias National Park & Preserve was our main adventure for the day. It happens to be the largest National Park in the U.S. and probably one, no one knows exists. It has a 16,390' mountain called Mt. Blackburn, and a 16,237' Mt. Sanford, plus Mt. Wrangell comes in at 14,163'. There are lots of glaciers within this park and as I understand a great heli-skiing place. We're camped on Rufus Creek; a beautiful spot. The road turns north again so who knows what may lie ahead; but, adventures, I'm sure are there to be had.

SATURDAY, AUGUST 26

Today will be our last day in Alaska; we've done and have seen a lot. Maybe tried to see too much, contrary to what I tell my grandkids. I'll tell them "you can't see or do it all, life is too short, but you can enjoy what you see and do."

I'd say coming back to this great north land is worth a fishing trip someday before I pass away. Ma is tired of being cold and wet, but she has had a good time in spite of it and has gained a new appreciation for our toasty warm solar home. We may exit Alaska, but Alaska will never exit us. It's a land like no other, and people like no other. They are here like Dean is here, you come to see, but it grabs you and won't let you go. It's vast and it's wild. It's what's embedded in our very soul.

We were driving in Wrangell-St. Elis N.P. and came upon a young man thumbing a ride. We were 30 to 40 miles from any civilization. I usually don't pick up hitchhikers but because of location it seemed the right thing to do. He was nine miles from his truck and wanted a ride to it. I remembered passing the truck. His wife was sitting on a log in a stream about 100 yards away. We couldn't haul both, so she stayed behind. They had been in the wilderness a week hunting Dall sheep. He said she was pretty excited because she had got her first. We found out that they lived on the same road that Dean lives on.

He came to Alaska about five years earlier, but called Alaska home. That's what this country does to you. You are thinking this is a young person's place and you may be right, but you're only as old as you feel. We'll be crossing the line again tomorrow, but not all lines are boundaries. It's just something to jump from one adventure to another. How much fun can a person endure? We'll find out.

Sunday, August 27

The Yukon, I'm guessing this is the feel Alaska used to be. No cruise ships, few tour busses, and few places that try to sell you something you don't need. I really like the Yukon. It's not as dramatic in scenery, but as beautiful as it needs to be, if compared to Alaska. Its remote, its wild and it's still the way God made it. The pace is slow here, I'm thinking, because there is little need to seek anything better. We stopped at a lake for lunch today and drove down a lane that ended next to the water. A lone loon was diving for food, eventually going out of our viewing area as it worked its way up the lake. The sun was out and the warmth felt good. I set my camera on the tripod and snapped a few pictures. I've snapped a lot of pictures on this trip, but none will capture what I have captured in my memory. It's the memories that will endure. The photos will bring those moments back to life. I'm really going to miss this country, I'm just now beginning to see what holds people to a place that the outside world thinks is inhabitable. Gold seekers are almost always disappointed, but those who seek the natural world seem to find joy and contentment. The gold seekers will eventually come and build their resorts, and bus the multitudes in and call it progress, but for now it's perfect. I'm glad I had the opportunity to see such a place. I built a fire at camp tonight. I thought of how Dad used to like campfires. I toasted marshmallows and had a hot chocolate, I thought of how Mom would have loved to take a trip like this; she would appreciate it more than anyone. The journey is only half over, so what's down the road I can only imagine. Each day is better than the last, that's the way life should be. If you're reading this and you are; the world is waiting, waiting for you.

Monday - Tuesday, August 28 - 29

Canyons! I've been in several in my lifetime. Today I've added another to my list, that would be Miles Canyon near Whitehorse, Yukon. The Yukon River flows through a narrow passage of basalt rock. Although this part of the river would be considered the headwaters, other rivers, farther upstream, come together to make the Yukon River what it is and that is one of the largest drainages in the world. It starts somewhere in British Columbia and flows through the Yukon, and then empties into the Bering Sea off the west coast of Alaska.

Some of us grew up in canyons and didn't know it. To a flatlander near Bellville, Ohio, Dean, as a kid, thought we lived in the mountains of Athens. We can't judge a canyon necessarily by its size, but by its character. Did you know that Palo Duro Canyon in western Texas is second only to the Grand Canyon in the volume of space it takes up? We misjudge a lot of things, at least that's what Teddi says I do. It's a learning process. Some even go through emotional canyons. As I've spoken to people that live in this far north land, they have told me of reasons why they live here. It's a new start for them and they say it has worked; they would never live anywhere else.

Tonight, I'm hoping to see what's above the earth as opposed to its depths, that would be the northern lights. We haven't seen any yet, mostly because we're asleep at two in the morning, but it's also been cloudy a lot. Not to mention, it's not really dark here very long in the summer. Maybe we'll have to come back in the dead of winter when nights are a little longer. I'm sure Ma thinks not. Well another good day, and another story by the campfire. We'll see you down the road somewhere tomorrow.

Wednesday, August 30

Have you ever felt like you are in the dark when the world around you seems enlightened? If you're hearing impaired, you probably know that feeling, but this is not a story about hearing, but seeing, and seeing some things can leave you speechless. Words cannot describe some of the things we've seen. Are you puzzled yet? Well, last night Ma and I hopped in our car around 10:30 PM and drove from our camp to a setting where we could look unobstructed toward the north. One of my goals for this trip was to see Denali and the other, the Aurora Borealis; both had two chances - slim and none. The first sighting happened, which would have been good enough; the second seemed dimmer. At 10:30 it's still light out. To top that off, the moon was out at about half-full. In our southeast Ohio world the moon rises in the evening and shines during the night, but here it set behind the mountains in the south. That was strange to me. Now that the moon was gone and the sun finally setting in the west, the stars started to come out. There is no pollution here, just clear, clean air. Kris would have a hay day with his telescope, with the Milky Way out in all its glory, staring down at us. To have a nearly clear sky, free of clouds, was a stroke of good fortune. The chances of seeing any Northern Lights this time of year was still that slim part I talked of earlier. We're looking at stars and watching some people pushing burning wood into the Yukon River, sort of like a flaming waterfall, that was interesting. It's getting to be around 12:00 midnight now; like I said, slim chances of seeing any lights. On a scale of one to nine, a lady at the visitor's center said if it happened it would only be a three in any magnitude. Unwavering, we're looking toward the north and I'm thinking I see a lighter glow, kind of like a high-powered light that shines back and forth in the sky to advertise something with to get your attention. Ma mentions a cloud moving in. I see a cloud building across the horizon but in a perfect arch. I'm thinking this is no normal cloud. It builds until it almost glows, then it starts to break apart and low and behold they streak vertical in the sky. No colors, but white towers moving across the sky like giant curtains folding. It would fade then would come back and show us another pattern. At around 1:00 in the morning the show was about over; we went back to our camper. Words cannot describe the Northern Lights, even at a three on the scale, so a nine would take your breath away. I'm blessed to see so much when I expected to see so little. Tonight, we're camped on the Rancheria River, our last night in the Yukon. The wonders never cease.

Thursday, August 31

Autumn is in the air, we can see it, feel it, and smell it. Our journey is taking us down the Cassiar Highway in northern British Columbia. It's the time of year I look forward to the most. The Aspen are beginning to display the yellow of their kind. The mountains are showing white on their crowns. One lane roads become ablaze with the reds, browns, and yellows as you gaze down their corridors with green showing between its tracks. The already fallen leaves are giving forth the scent only autumn can bring. Did I say it's still August here? I'm thinking I'll get three months of moments such as this before winter sets in at our southeast Ohio home; at least that's the plan. There is water flowing by our camp tonight, two rivers being yoked together in front of our door as they flow toward the Pacific Ocean. It's a most tranquil spot to rest before setting out for what lies ahead; the ahead always beckons us, but that's good. It's the adventure that drives our soul.

Friday, September 1

Waterfalls, which would be today's theme. As a kid growing up, the world seemed very big. I remember Sharon, Jeff, Jo, Mark, Barb and myself playing in an area below our house near the old coal tipple. It was a small stream fed by water from coal mines farther upstream. At one point it had to drop over a rock that was not quite a fall, but close enough; the younger ones called it Root Beer Falls; the sulfur in the water gave it the color, so the name. Today we're in Stewart, British Columbia with glaciers hanging off nearly vertical mountains next to the sea. It's normally a rainy area, but recent storms have created a site I may never see again. Water is flowing at every crevice, dropping through the air to land again on rocks below; not just a few feet, but hundreds to a thousand feet. There are torrents of water flowing out of the base of glaciers to create streams, lakes, rivers. The water is flowing so fast that a mist rises above it. The river was lapping at the edge of the highway. I've taken pictures, but they will never capture what was around me. I'm humbled by the sites I've seen. We also saw two black bears today, one paying the ultimate price by a motorized machine. Yes, sad, but bears and man don't mix well. I'm glad there are areas where they don't have to.

We are still pretty much in the middle of

nowhere, but we're approaching civilization again. I'm going to miss this natural world, but stories will still unfold I know. We'll see what is down the road, join us as we go.

Saturday, September 2

Have you ever been a farmer, or thought of being one? Today's journey took us past the first we have seen in many weeks, that is if you consider having goats and one pig a farm. I thought it strange to see a pig this far north. I'm sure, before winter, it will be a table setting with an apple in its mouth around Thanksgiving. For some reason potato farming entered my mind. If you have never planted potatoes with my Dad, you have been short changed in one of life's most memorable moments. I'll try to make this as short as I can. First, you bring home a bag of seed potatoes that's big enough to put in the cellar to last through the winter. Then, you cut each potato into pieces that have just one or two eyes; simple, right? Dad may catch one of yours that fail the two-eye test, then you have done it all wrong. That was the easy part. Now the marking out part with the plow, that is plowing a row for the potatoes to be thrown in at just the precise distance of spacing between each cut potato. If you're the tractor driver, the row is never straight enough, or if you're on the plow, which was a horse-drawn marking out type, it's your fault the rows are not straight enough. Once the potatoes were thrown in the ditch, usually all wrong, the fertilizer was added; too much or too little seemed to be the way I would do it. Covering the potatoes with dirt was next, once again too much cover or not enough was my lot. Oh, the joys of farming. Guess why I went off to join the Army.

Today we saw more sockeye salmon with a bear close by in the brush. We also saw another bear down the road. A fox also made an appearance. It's been a good day.

Sunday, September 3

Have you ever done any exploring? As a kid

I remember exploring every inch of the back forty. Sometimes on purpose, but mostly, looking for cows to bring down to milk. To this day I can tell you where each clump of brush, berry patch, apple, hickory, or walnut, where the largest oak tree or the best spring was. I can tell you where I saw a porcupine. All that seems natural to me, but exploring can come other ways; like learning to spell. I was thinking about shooting hoops when that was taught. When grammar was taught, I'm sure I was looking out the window as the teacher was presenting that. I'm thinking whatever your niche is, explore it. Captain James Cook made a trip through western Canada and Alaska in the 1700's on foot. Seeing how hard it would be to go anywhere by foot in this country, I'm thinking he was the ultimate explorer. Two months have flown by but we're still exploring. Tomorrow we will be back in the lower 48. From now on we'll be seeing most of what everyone else sees as they pass, but I'm hoping to glean some more good ventures out of some familiar territory. We have driven so many miles that a drive across the U.S. will seem like as a drive from Athens to Columbus used to feel like. Contrary to what you may think, I look forward to every mile. Maybe I'll try to communicate with humans other than Teddi again. Who knows, it's worth a try. We saw another black bear today.

Monday, September 4

Rides can be exciting, ask the grandkids. They seek out all the thrill rides at amusement parks. I'm sure Wesley hasn't missed any of the biggest, fastest, or twistiest ones the park has to offer. I'll tell you of a thrill ride I had about sixty years ago. No waiting in line to be carried to the top for this one, I didn't even have to pay. It begins with a soapbox car Larry made from a previous story. It had fairly wide spaced front wheels but the back ones close together. You sat on a box, thus its name, and placed your feet on the board that held the front wheels. It hinged in the middle so you steered by pushing with either your right or left foot to guide where you wanted to go. It had a good weight distribution so on really fast turns the back end would slide out a little. It was also kind of heavy, so pulling it uphill took some effort. Those were the strip mining years at home on Long Run. It was summer and they had been hauling coal from the hill where they were stripping, down to Long Run, and beyond. Near the bottom, a sharp curve came into play because of a rock ledge next to the road. It was Sunday and in those days no one worked on Sunday. They had been hauling all week so the road was smooth with about one-half inch of dust on top of the road. I had pulled the cart to the top and made a really fun run to the bottom. It was so much fun I decided to do it again. Normally one run took most of my energy, but this was so much fun I decided to do it again. So back to the top and I start out again; gaining speed, I approached the curve with the back end sliding out like a Torch Raceway stock car; this is fun stuff. The curve also blinds the road as you approach

Long Run. The rock ledge is straight ahead. I'm moving as fast as four wheels and gravity can take me. The back end is hanging out and I'm halfway through the curve when I spot a dump truck coming up the hill; not a good sign. Instinctively, I steer hard to the left, air 15-20 feet off the rock ledge, land in the middle of Long Run road, then bounce to the middle of Long Run creek. The driver stopping his truck, and surely expecting the worst, runs over to where I'm at and asked if I was OK. I was OK, actually more than OK, I had the ride of a lifetime and I had survived. I get goosebumps just thinking about it. Some memories are great; today's endeavor not so much. We had a long drive in southern British Columbia with smoke hanging heavy in the air and bumper to bumper traffic. It's also Monday, Labor Day, what was I thinking. Dates have had little meaning since we left home. We also went from 40 degrees to 99 degrees in the Frazer River canyon; just today. Oh, to be back in Alaska, listening to rain on our roof. With hesitancy, I'll say it's good to be back on home turf. We have a nice camp at Mt. Baker in Washington tonight. No more Loonies or Toonies, just George. We'll see you on the summit of Mt. Baker tomorrow. We have telephoto.

Tuesday, September 5

This is the day I've dreaded for a while, driving to where traffic never, ever, ceases to go by. If you're in the flow, it's like lemmings going over a cliff; if you want to get in the flow, good luck with that, if you want to get out of the flow, there's plenty that will push you to the brink. I love city driving, just ask Teddi. Fifty years ago we lived in Seattle and it wasn't so bad, I never gave it much thought. It was a little crowded around 4:00 to 6:00 but tolerable, today we're 80 miles away and its bumper to bumper and not even rush hour. Oh, to be back in Alaska where the only thing on the road is a bear, or even in southeast Ohio where gridlock is a four-car backup. I know there's a reason for migrating to the big cities, jobs obviously, but the brochures also say how exciting and perfect it is. I'm sure the same people wrote the ones for the cruise ships and Alaska, too. A place where the sun always shines and whales are spotted in every bay, and fish jump right into your boat. I've been to a lot of places in North America and every village, town, and city has the same thing. I just like a little less of everything and time to enjoy the things I have; not setting on pavement waiting to do it. Already, I'm acting like the people around me, forgive me. Tomorrow, after a good night's sleep, I'm sure I'll be OK. We may check if the spot we met at still exists, probably not, but it will be fun trying. We've come a long way from this spot 49 years ago; we've had a family, traveled, but mostly we've experienced and lived life as best we could. You can never go back, so our option is to keep going on. We walked on the beach at Whidbey Island this evening, as we walked on similar beaches many years ago.

Wednesday, September 6

Today we made our way to the site of our meeting place those many years ago. It's now a huge warehouse for some trucking outfit, how unromantic can that be. Like I said, you can't go back, but all was not lost as Boeing's Museum of Flight was a gem I didn't expect and just half a runway up the road. I would put it on equal status with the Air Force Museum in Dayton, Ohio, different in presentation but very interesting. I saw my first 3-D movie. It showed the makeup of our nuclear aircraft carrier; very informative. We also had our first trip back to downtown Seattle in a long time. It has grown fifty-fold and still growing like no other city I've seen. Interstate 5, I can't begin to describe the nightmare, a city with a major problem. It's a city that runs from Canada to below Olympia, no kidding. There's no sun today. Smoke, not clouds, have shut down my solar panels; no mountains to be seen either. I forgot to mention about Ma walking out on Deception Pass Bridge yesterday. It's really high above Puget Sound. She got a little freaked out and I thought I was going to have to carry her back, she's losing her edge. Maybe because of a meager hand rail, cars and trucks going by just inches away, and the bridge moving a tad with the flow of traffic; a nice view though. My having to drive I-5 was payback for laughing at her. Let the journey continue.

THURSDAY, SEPTEMBER 7

We were looking at snow caves at Mt. Baker the other day and it got me thinking of different snow scenes I've seen over the years. The storm of 1950 (I think) was the most I've seen in Ohio. As a kid I remember jumping off the cellar into the snow. In my teen years, the hill at Clarks Chapel drifted quite deep. I've seen a lot of snow and ice on this trip, more than I'll ever see again, but the most interesting snow were the snow rolls where we lived on Coolville Ridge. New, wet snow and heavy winds made rolls one to two feet in diameter and hollow in the center. They were everywhere like small rolls of hay; really cool stuff.

I'll never forget skiing Monarch Pass in Colorado with Josh. We had an all-night snow followed by snow all day while we were skiing. I remember Josh taking off in front of me on a run and the snow actually rolling over the top of his head. Each run was as if no one had been there before, powder snow at its finest. That afternoon I was sure I couldn't do another run because my legs were a little tired, when Josh would say, one more. After five, one mores, and legs like Jell-O, we finally called it quits. We both knew that was a special day.

I remember sledding with Mark on the hill up road from our house. We made a kind of bobsled run through some apple trees. By ourselves each run went really well, but then we tried to go tandem with Mark on top. At the second curve, the snow gave way under our combined weight, the sled stopped, Mark didn't. He went flying into an apple tree trunk; I thought he had broken his collarbone. He didn't, but the sledding day ended. There's always a drawback to everything.

Our trip down the Oregon coast doesn't have snow but we've brought much needed rain; that's the way the Oregon coast is supposed to be like. I know, everyone wants sun, but with the fires burning everywhere, they're ready for typical Northwest weather. The road we're on is the same path we took forty-nine years ago on our honeymoon. The wife is still just as beautiful and nice as she was then. That first trip we got soaked by rain as we were camping in a not so good of a tent, but a hard shell over our head is keeping us dry and toasty this time. It won't be as good a story as forty-nine years ago, but each story is good.

Tonight I had the same feeling as Teddi did when going to the blueberry festival in Alaska. We made a fairly long drive to the Tillamook Cheese Factory in Oregon for their chocolate ice cream. We waited in line hoping to be waited on before they closed. I was feeling good that we beat the closing deadline and the young man took my order. Teddi went with some order that probably had blueberries in it, but I just wanted plain chocolate; it's so good. The waiter then say's *no chocolate* - a day of anticipation down the tubes in two words. Ice cream is good in about any flavor; I'm still trying to convince myself. This was a sad day.

FRIDAY – SUNDAY, SEPTEMBER 8 -10

The family I grew up with has more stories to tell than most book stores. Two days with Larry recovered a lot that I knew but some I had not heard before. That happens about every time some of us get together. Even if we have heard them, one more item gets added that wasn't in previous renditions. Larry's story of fishing with a ball peen hammer was one I hadn't heard before; then his stories predate a lot of mine. I'm still just a pup. As I'm writing this a major story is unfolding in Florida for two sisters and a daughter. A huge hurricane is bearing down on their homes. They went to a safer part of the state but worries always travel with you. My prayer is that their stories will be good ones that they won't mind telling us some time in the future.

Today's journey took us through smoke and traffic away from the interstate highway; then by a lot of sagebrush to an off the main road camp. We lost an hour in the process because of the time change. We're just a few days in the lower forty-eight and I'm already back in a timed world; how sad is that. We have another flowing stream to sleep by tonight; may the ones in Florida sleep as well as I will and awake to good news.

Monday, September 11

Storms: we have all been through storms in our lives at one time or another; those emotional roller coasters that help identify who we are. I could talk about the human side but that would be a little uncomfortable for most, so let's talk of natural storms. I've mentioned the 1950 snow storm and snow roll episode but others come to mind. As a kid growing up any thunderstorm at our house had potential for water entering our living space. As rains lingered, cars had to be moved to a higher location, in general a real pain, but it also meant good swimming, indoors or out. If the water was indoors then that triggered a major cleanup afterwards; that was not fun. In a recent year a storm rolled through the home place when Mom was living there by herself. Some small lake upstream in back of the house washed its retainer out and brought dirt and gravel downstream; enough to fill Coal Branch completely up. I stood on the bridge and poked in the water before wading across to verify my fears; thinking I would have to rent a backhoe to clean it out. Darkness was approaching and water receding, so I came back the following morning. To my astonishment the water was back to normal and all, I mean all, the rock and gravel was gone. Nothing remained that represented any dirt had filled that stream. When our science books talk of the earth's time frame in development, I'm thinking they are way off. It could have happened over night. So I see different than the science books, after that episode.

A snow skiing trip took me to Stevens Pass, Washington one weekend. I was camped in my gold, and cream, 4 doors, 1958 Chevrolet Belair with the back seat removed and a bed placed that protruded into the trunk area. Ski mobiles come in all shapes and sizes. The day before I was skiing Mission Ridge near Wenatchee and had a good day. I was to spend the night at a campground nearer Stevens Pass as to get first tracks the next day. I slept like a contented baby. I kept waiting for the early morning light but it just seemed later than usual, I never carry a watch. After a while, I realized I couldn't see out. I went to open the door and found a lot of resistance. Snow, new snow had fallen overnight and a lot of it. I'm seeing about 18 to 20 inches of great powder and I'm buried in a campground, miles from the main highway, and it's up a grade. You're right; I'm the only one there. My Belair was not just a ski mobile but a virtual snow mobile, as it pushed snow driving out. Yes; it was great skiing.

Watching and hearing trees break during a derecho was kind of interesting. Hearing the sirens go off at Kris's house in Cedarville kind of gets you excited. I've others but this is too long as it is. We are camped at Craters of the Moon in Idaho tonight. This would have been a storm to see live as it was happening.

TUESDAY, SEPTEMBER 12

Today we're passing through a land with few trees. It's a high desert area of Idaho, mostly rock and sagebrush, but it has a beauty about it. It's different than the towering cedars of the coast of Washington, but nothing's ever the same; as it should be. Beauty is everywhere. The elm tree that grew in our front yard was large and full. It too had beauty. The stories that took place under its branches could fill a book. It provided shade, it was a garage, it was where the school bus turned around, it was where all cars and tractors were worked on, it was where anger was vented at times, it was a turnaround point for lost travelers, and it was the best basketball arena in the world. It also sheltered a coal pile, and had a swing that could put you into orbit. Bicycles could jump ramp to ramp under its branches or allow first timers to learn the art. The elm tree was a part of each and every one of us. From the great pickup basketball games on a hot Sunday afternoon to trying to dribble on frozen, rutted, dirt in the winter, maybe playing by your lonesome. Each of us has a story. Those were great moments as I look back. The elm tree no longer stands, but oh, the stories each branch witnessed. We blend with nature whether we think so or not. What drives the stories in your life; it doesn't have to be a tree, but something needs to shelter a good story.

Not so many years ago Pete and I made a ski trip to Montana, Idaho, and Wyoming. We ended our venture at Jackson Hole near the Grand

Teton National Park. That of itself would have been a good story, but this is about what happened afterwards. The day started like any ski day, an early rise as to catch any new snow if any has fallen, catch as many runs as possible before your legs go south, and hope you don't ski over a cliff. Winter days are short in North Country, so we skied through lunch expecting to eat before heading east. It was a good ski day. Aren't they all? We packed our gear into the car and headed to find a restaurant. A few hours of daylight was left, so we bought some sandwich food instead and decided to head toward Yellowstone as far as the road was open. The snow was only a few feet deep as we left Jackson Hole, but with each passing mile became deeper. The Grand Tetons are spectacular in the winter. The road ended at Colter Bay on Jackson Lake. A trench was dug out to the lodge area. There were no sign of humans anywhere; the snow around eight feet deep on each side. At a pull out we had only enough room to get the car off the road. There was a wall of snow between us and the Snake River, so we kicked steps in it to get to the top. We sat down with our food and looked across the frozen, snow covered water, with mountains rising in the background; a small island not far away with evergreens standing tall. It was breathtaking in itself, but as we sat in silence, a bald eagle landed on top of a fir tree, and then two moose walked about a hundred yards out on the ice and stopped. We're watching this beautiful site when an otter below us gains our attention at the only unfrozen spot on the river. We do not believe what we're seeing, but it only gets better. The sun is beginning to set behind 11,258' Eagles Nest Peak with 12,605' Mt. Moran just to its left. The scattered clouds that are aloft come alive with a reddish glow against a darkening blue background. We sat in silence, taking in this amazing site that was unfolding before us. It took a while before we could say anything. Darkness settled over us as we eased our way back to the car. This event could never be duplicated. I'm glad I could share it with my son. I hope someday he can share a moment as this with his.

WEDNESDAY, SEPTEMBER 13

Dirt roads: the majority of people in this nation have never seen a dirt road. Our populous live either on the east coast or the west coast, where lanes of asphalt reach eight or more lanes wide. What they see on their drives is not a scenic country path, but probably the rear end of another car and that car has the same view. My Explorer just registered over one quarter of a million miles, but the day I drove it off the lot, new, it never looked as clean as the used ones as I see on the road today. Today, we found ourselves on yet another dirt road between the Grand Tetons and Yellowstone, it followed Pole Cat Creek. That road will take you to Idaho if you so desire. About three other cars were passed as we traveled a short distance before turning around. We saw birds of different sorts, six deer, and a red fox. The scenery was beautiful. We spotted flowers where a forest fire had burned a year or two earlier. The blackened area is coming back to life. Tonight we had our delayed anniversary dinner at the plush Jackson Lake Lodge; we were in Seward, Alaska on that memorable day. Tonight there was prime rib for me and trout for Ma. We saw moose and elk after dinner as the sun was setting over the Tetons. An early morning walk presented chukars (that's a bird) and a large, beautiful red fox. We saw few people, few cars, but on these dirt paths we saw more than just the red of tail lights. We made a good choice today. I'm hoping after tomorrow we can say the same.

Thursday, September 14

The other day I saw a sign that read "watch for children in road." This was a rural setting where we were, but it's been a while since I've seen free-range kids; not since the likes of my four younger siblings have kids roamed so free. They have a story I can't pass up. I was around but not a part of their trip to Timbuktu. Sister Jo has the correct details, but I'll pass it along, for records sake, of what little I know about the trip from Jo's telling. Mark probably asked where Timbuktu was. Jeff said he knew exactly where it was; we're talking kids at the age of three to seven or so. Barb was on her tricycle, Jo with the pony, Jeff leading the Pac, and Mark probably mutilating wildlife as they begin their journey to Timbuktu. Sometime that afternoon Mom receives a phone call from her sister Naomi. Naomi asks Mom if she knows where her kids were; of course she did, "they are outside playing" was Moms reply. A short silence on the phone; Then Naomi says, "They're at my house." Now Jeff, as leader of the Pac, recognizing Naomi's house on their trip to Timbuktu, and realizing how tired his crew was, stopped for a break and a drink of water. Like many journeys that don't reach their destination, theirs's was also halted. Naomi lived four to five miles from our home. Dad was working and had the car. They were brought home after he got off work. Beth had to ride the pony home; she was not a happy camper. I've been to a lot of places, but like my brothers and sisters, I haven't made it to Timbuktu either. That happened when the world was a lot safer, and kids could roam free. Oh: I wish I could say that today but I can't. Someday, maybe someday we can safely take the trip to Timbuktu.

Our travels today took us to the more common spots and pull offs of the beautiful Grand Teton National Park. We visited String and Jenny lakes, the Snake River, and spotted a moose and her young near a place called Moose. We saw a movie at the visitor's center while a rain storm passed. We drove up yet another dirt road to Jackson Lake; a good day.

Friday, September 15

We've been in a lot of Parks, and camping areas where homes or buildings are never seen. We stopped many times to trek to a vantage point or a spot of scenic beauty. Just about all these places are observed after walking a dirt path. Paths normally lead to better things; like a trip to the outhouse when growing up. One always feels better after that walk. That path also gave you the opportunity to pick up walnuts or check for ripe hazelnuts; even blackberries grew along this dirt path. Paths can make for unique encounters.

Once when living on Coolville Ridge, I was following a path next to the hayfields and woods edge. I heard a sound a distance behind me, so I stopped. A young doe was on the same path. I eased into a bush beside me, but still on the path, so she couldn't see me. To my surprise she walked right next to me and actually brushed my leg. The wind kept my scent away and silence on my part led to this unique experience.

A path up Black Butte in Oregon brought out more than Heidi thought she had in her; or Lea's trek to the springs of the Metolius River at the western family Roundup. A hike in the mountains normally proves that the rougher the path, the better the view. The bike path in Athens that finishes the marathon wasn't dirt, but it made for a great moment as I crossed the line. Paths, generally lead to a more rewarding place, so get off the crowded highway and find a good path; you'll be glad you did.

SATURDAY, SEPTEMBER 16

Another story for old times' sake was the day we got television; the second saddest day in my life. Sometimes we're just born at the wrong time. A lot goes into getting a picture in a box setting in the living room. Because of people like me, the development of TV escalated like no other product and here's the reason why. For us get a picture in that box, an antenna had to be placed for reception to occur; then wire was run to connect the box with the antenna. Hills seem to be detrimental to the process. We placed ours a quarter of a mile from the house over a stripped hillside that exposed a vertical rock wall to an elevation that took oxygen to survive, plus three fences had to be navigated, try finding barbed wire in the dark. Yes, the connecting wire; two strands of thread placed at just the precise distance from each other as to not allow interference to occur were put in place. The high Tec product used here was a hair roller made from plastic (it probably has a better name) to separate the wires. We never put enough along the route, so a hush of any breeze would twist the wires and then crossing would occur; not good for reception. I carried a long stick with me to uncross the wires; as they were elevated as not to hang anyone that passed by. The pole that held the antenna was fastened to a long wooden post buried in the ground. The fastening product here was just wire rapped around the pole to keep it upright. Again, any breeze that occurred would turn the antenna from the precise direction that it had to be directed toward, to get a picture. Being in shape was not an issue I had to contend with from the day the TV was installed. Once all this was in place and tuned to its finest, at its very best, it was like watching a blizzard occur during any broadcast. Like I said, it was the second saddest day of my life.

SUNDAY, SEPTEMBER 17

Have you ever rode in a hearse; the vehicle that carries a person to the burial ground? You probably haven't unless you work for a mortuary or a part of my family. Ronnie bought a 1948 Buick Roadmaster, straight eight cylinders, column shift, with velour interior, and black of course while going to Williams College. Now there was a car with some room and a really soft ride. It also draws attention. It became a multi-purpose vehicle way before its time. It hauled people of course, but it also hauled hay and even my 4-H steer to the county fair. Ronnie wasn't very happy about that; with a steer, in confinement and motion, plus a little nervous about the whole thing, brings out the worst in an animal - that would be a bowel issue. Messy will be the word I'll use. I'm not sure if the smell ever left, but we did get it clean, not easy to do with plush velour. Nothing is too good for a prize-winning animal. Go to Kentucky sometime if you don't believe that. Why I'm telling you this I'm not sure, other than life has really been fun and sometimes a little unorthodox.

Monday, September 18

After spending time in Colorado at Josh and Megan's, we are taking a more direct route toward home; not the wandering path we usually do. Cold weather is looming over the horizon and some preparation should be taken for a winter season. Eleven weeks have passed since our leaving. It has gone by way too fast. Yes, it's good to be heading back to our home, but traveling is in our blood. Ma loves to see different things and places, she has the heart of a Gypsy. We have had a year without a real summer, so winter may seem a little longer which is down my alley, as I'm not much of a hot weather person. I still have stories to tell but it may take another trip for the inspiration. Larry has a long list of his own just waiting for the right time to put it in print. I'm sure each of you has stories that should be passed down. All you need is a little nudge. Ours is the open road. What's yours?

ABOUT THE AUTHOR

If you are looking for the author, John Williams, you won't find him in the office writing. He may be trekking a nearby hiking trail or floating in his canoe or kayak on one of the beautiful lakes that surround his Appalachian foothills home. If not there, jump on your bicycle and find a nearby trail, he may be wrapped around a tree somewhere and in need of your help. Teddi, his wife of 50 years, will tell you to take your time. Four children, all grown, made a break for it and put roots in different parts of our beautiful country. The seven grandkids don't know what he looks like.

Go to the nearest locally owned coffee shop and just by chance he may be there. He will be the only one with a pencil and paper.

www.ingramcontent.com/pod-product-compliance
Lightning Source LLC
Chambersburg PA
CBHW031352160426
42811CB00092B/14